Copyright © 2017

Chakerah Brown

First Printing

Memoirs of a Broken Butterfly: Queen Rose'

Bethune Publishing House
The Bethune Group
All rights reserved, including the right to reproduce this work in any form whatsoever without written permission from the publisher, except for brief passages in connection with a review. Photographs may not be reproduced without permission of the owner.

For information write:
Bethune Publishing House, Inc.
P. O. Box 2008
Daytona Beach, FL 32115-2008
docbethune@tbginc.org

Jacket designed by John-Mark McLeod
J2maginations, LLC
J2maginations@gmail.com

Book design and page layout by
Bethune Publishing House, Inc.

Printed in the United States of America
Library of Congress Control Number: 2017952964
ISBN: 978-1-946566-0 -8

Memoirs of a Broken Butterfly
'Queen Rose'

Composed by
Chakerah Brown

Dedicated To...

To Aysha

Thanks for being my biggest inspiration and keeping me alive at some of my darkest moments in my life. I love you and I appreciate you for being the best little sister ever. I want you to continue to become the best woman I know you can be.

To Trey

The second love of my life, my biggest headache but the other half of my heart. You made my life so much better and without you I don't know where I would be in life. Continue to be a great young man.

Nigel

The first love of my life, my best friend, my father figure, my cousin, I love you more than I can express and I want you to know that to me you're perfect.

Grandma & Grandma Scott

Thanks for always being there when I need you most. I love you more than I can ever tell you. I hope one day to make you both very, very, proud in something that I do.

Aunt Kim & Uncle Derrick

Thanks for being my biggest supporters and always being the ones, I can talk too. I thank you for all that you've done for me in my life and one day I hope to repay you both for all of your generosity. Love you both so, so, so, so, much!!!

Last but not least,

Bella Bean

My Sugar dumpling, my greatest blessing, my whole heart, my spoiled princess, I love you more than you'll ever know and I thank your daddy for letting you be in my life. I want you to know that you make my life worth living and without you, life would be boring. Love you Muffin.

Acknowledgements

I would like to personally and gratefully acknowledge the various people who have helped me on this journey of expressing my true feelings on paper. First, I would like to thank God for giving me the gift of poetic expression. Secondly, my mother for giving me life so that I can share my gift with the world. Thirdly, Daddy Ty for taking the place that my father didn't want. I thank you for being supportive throughout my life even when I was wrong. Valerie, Icis, Key and Kristina for always having my back and giving me words of encouragement no matter what time of day or night it is, I love and appreciate you all forthat.

Tattoo Daddy Mike (Mykal Rock) for being a father figure to me when I needed you most I am forever in debt to you. The best English teacher in the world Dr. Tennial the person that told me never to stop writing no matter what, I am very grateful for your words of wisdom. My HunBun Brena, girl you been my A1 since Day 1 and you've NEVER folded. You are the true meaning of the word family but your truly one of my best friends. Quatro, even though you get on my nerves I thank you for the Support. Cookie, my sister from another mother, thanks for coming into my life and being the older sister that I never had. To all my aunts and uncles who have contributed any advice, or a listening ear thank you.

To my brother Taylor you get on my nerves, but I couldn't ask for a better big brother, love you. Nick, my headache, the person that has inspired several of the poems in this book. Thank for you the good, the bad and the ugly. I couldn't have done it without you. Cousins, friends, random people that have lent a helpful word of advice I thank and appreciate you. If I forgot you, blame the mind not the heart.

A Caterpillar goes through Metamorphosis to become a Butterfly, but once that butterfly is broken you get its memoirs... Welcome to "Memoirs of a Broken Butterfly".

Black Lives Matter

When We Say Black Lives Matter
It's Not That All Lives Don't.
It's Just We Were Born
With A Target On Our Backs.

It's Not That Cop Lives Don't Matter,
But To The Cops, Our Lives Don't Matter.
It's Not That All People Don't Have A Purpose,
But Y'all Killing Our Black Men
And It's Purposeless.

Mothers Crying, They Sons Are Dying
At The Hands Of The Ones
That's Supposed To Serve And Protect,
But Instead Their Knees Are In Our Backs, And Their
Hands Around Our Necks.

Shot Down In The Street, Recordings
For The Whole World Too See.
Injustice Everyday And Yet
The Crookedness Walks Free.

When We March In The Streets
It's Not To Be A Threat,
But This Melanin We Possess
Make The Weak Tremble With Fear
And They Start To Stress.

Is It Cause Our Minds And Third Eye
Is Awake And There's No Longer A Debate That
Black Lives Matter?

The Perceptions of a Little Black Girl

So what I was born in the hood,

That doesn't mean I can't speak proper English,

Yes I can read,

Not all black children are illiterate,

No I don't have to steal,

Don't you know that's a sin?

Yes I know about Jesus,

What you think my mother's the devil's advocate?

No I don't have to share clothes

My parents have jobs

Yes I value my education,

Are you intimidated?

Are you upset because I'm intelligent?

(Laughing) You really thought I was just another black girl from the hood?

(Smirking) Are you agitated because I'm proving all your stereotypes about me wrong?

Or has that Smile on your face been wiped off because I'm too intelligent for your liking?

Get used to it, because one day your gonna
See my name in lights,

Any more questions or can we end this imperceptible phone call, I have things to do…

That don't include sitting here entertaining you.

It's been really nice chatting with you, but my future is on the other line.

Have a blessed day, when you're not so ignorant we can finish this on my time.

Prostitute Done

There once was a girl

Who was all alone in the world

She needed attention and affection

She ran the streets all night

'Til she found a man

Who told her she could have a man whatever she liked

She took his word for it and started working for him

It was good at first

The money as amazing, until she made him angry

And he showed his frustration,

He hither and beat her until she could take no more.

She decided it was time to get out

She went to her man.

He told her she couldn't leave him

She put a gun to her head.

Another trigger pulled…Another female gone

And another pimp on the run

O yea and another prostitute done…

Innocence Taken

Stop is the only word she could scream before he entered her innocence which causes her to

have bad dreams....

He took her childhood and caused her to grow up fast and now she's on the wrong track...

Only fifteen living the fast life, experiencing all the wrong things at the wrong time...

She feels empty and lonely inside and everyday she wakes up praying to die...

Why did he have to do this to me is a question she constantly asks with answers to no avail.

Wishing she could go back to that dreadful day....

That day when her innocence was taken away.

No More Abuse Deep dark secrets sit on his lips and cloud his mind...

How can he open his mouth and face his fears?

He wears sunglasses and long-sleeved clothes to hide the Scars and bruises...

Pain inflicted by the ones who are supposed to protect him from the hurt of the world...

He locks himself in the school stall too hide his tears from his friends and peers...

He thinks about giving up, he feels like he can't take the senseless beatings...

The punches too face and the kicks to his back and shin...

The pain is unbearable and undesirable....

Just as he went to hang himself he heard a voice that said "Don't worry my child for I am

always with you."

He looked up and saw a bright light....

From that moment on he was never abused again...

I AM A STRONG SUPPORTER OF PEOPLE AGAINST CHILD ABUSE

Signs

Trying to hide behind the reality of her deepest, darkest fears,

Shades on her face hiding her never ending tears,

Eyes blacked and lip busted by the one she most trusted,

Could it be he never loved and he only lusted?

In the beginning, it was sweet like paradise,

Everything was lovely and nice,

Self-Esteem feeling low,

Mind telling her to go,

But out of fear she refuses to run,

Even though she knows the time to leave has come,

Trying to gain the mental capacity to leave and never turn back,

Make a new path and find a new track,

How could she have been so blind to his fury?

Got her throwing the kids clothes in a suitcase in a hurry.

Daydreaming of a brighter future with a peace of mind.

Concluding right now is the perfect time and the rainbow in the sky was the perfect sign.

A House Is Not a Home

In a place where the voices never seem to stop raising anger never seems to cease and the tears never seem too stop falling...

In a room where the glass is shattered off the mirror due to a forceful impact of a door being slammed, jumping at every sudden movement...

In a dark closet where my anxiety increases with every deep breath and every curse word that's spoken into the air...

On a porch where all I see is empty alcohol bottles and cigarette buds filling the floor showing the way people tried to drink and smoke away their sorrow...

In a corner looking out at my surroundings not liking what I see, bleeding on the inside and crying on the Out...

Walking out in the peaceful cold to try and regain my composure trying to keep my thoughts to myself...

Pacing up and down the street with my headphones in my ear trying to keep the insanity Out ...

Isolating myself from the stupidity of the ones closest too me kicking up dust as I look over my shoulder...

Breaking down mentally while my strength slowly deteriorates... I don't know where to go or who to turn too...

Anger is clouding my Outer air and it seems too pollute my lungs and fill my insides with burning anguish...

A House Is Not A Home...

The Aftermath

Puzzle pieces and ripped pieces of paper

Broken glass and butcher knives scattered over the floor

Ripped and shredded clothes

Thrown shoes that put holes in the wall

Torn up pictures across the bathroom trailing to the kid's room.

All of these are remembrances of last night's argument that turned physical

Words were spoken that weren't meant and undefined actions were proposed.

Lipstick and mascara Smears across the banister and stairs

Wait is that a bullet hole?

Picture frames lying without pictures of our undying infatuation for one another.

Rings hidden in kitchen drawers and there's no more "I love yous" spoken

The room is silent and I'm debating whether to lock up and throw away the key.

This is the aftermath.

Married to the Devil/ Sleeping With the Enemy

So the man you're in love with has a nickname and no it's not Ike, Joe, or Harpo but it's Something just as bad You've been married to the devil and sleeping with the enemy and you feel cursed but you don't know why Loving him isn't easy and you know that but you feel like you can change him, I don't know why you feel that way,

But You've been married to the devil and sleeping with the enemy and you're unhappy but you don't know why So the man you're in love with is the devil and you're sleeping with the enemy and you feel cursed but you don't know why…

Unhated Daughter

They Say A Father Is Supposed Too Be A Girls First Love, The One To Show Her Off And Shower Her In Hugs.

The Man Too Teach Her About Boys And Tell Her Too Stay Away From Drugs. Life Gave Me Two People Saying Kerah That's A Blessing

But Real Life This Shit Got Me Stressing.

Going Against The Curve. Mistreated By What's Supposed To Be The Center Of My World... Instead The Physical, Mental, And Verbal Abuse Never Seems Too Stop...

Hearing Going Out And The Tears Forever Drop. This Feeling Of Being Unwanted And Unloved Makes My Heart Constantly Break, Can't I Just Be Great And Have A Break?

I Wasn't Asked To Be Made Let Alone Betrayed. Can Someone Help Me Figure Out The Secrets To Be A Daughter That's Not Hated?

01/07/2017

Letter to my Mother

Dear Mother,

"Sometimes I feel like a motherless child" is a song that constantly clouds my mind.... Did she really want me is a question that I ask myself all the time... Passing me off to others, having two more and then showing her true colors.... Making me feel unworthy and unwanted.... Kind of like a rose that's been wilted....

Feeling shut out by the one that's supposed to love me the most, lost like a paddle without a boat.... What do I have to do for her to love and want me'? Does she wish she would've aborted me or does she resent me because of my daddy? Needing answers to questions unasked, maybe that's why I acted out in my past.... Maybe I should reach out to my dad.... Wait, hold up, what's that? More like who's that? Nothing but his back is what I've seen... No don't get me wrong I know his name and face.... We're just not in a good place....

Giving more love to my sister and brother... Making me feel empty, this is a letter to my mother.

Letter to My Unborn

Dear Angel Looking Over Mommy and Daddy,

I'm sorry that you never got the chance to experience this world out here, but trust me

baby it was for your best interest my dear. An innocent face I never got to see, a sweet laugh

that I never got to hear, mommy giving you back to GOD was my worst fear, but see daddy wasn't ready for you to be here. And no my child you were not a mistake you just came at the most inopportune time losing you feels like the worst committed crime. I wish I could wake up and see your smile but trust me baby during another time and place we will be reunited.

Rest easy my dear child. This is a letter to my unborn.

Diary of a Mistress

You Go Too Her Knowing You Just Left Me,

You Kiss Her Knowing You Just Kissed Me,

Touching on Her Body While You Think of Me,

My Taste Lingering On Your Lips,

While You Take her for a Ride She'll Never Forget,

Living Two Separate Lives Got You Smoking Cigarettes,

You Got A Wife And A Mistress, Tell Me Baby Do You Even Know The Difference?

Why Does Love Hurt So Bad

Love Hurts So Much Because We Expect the Impossible,

Somebody to Love, Cherish and Respect Us Mentally, Emotionally, Physically, And Spiritually

Love Hurts So Much Because We Give Our Hearts to Somebody Wishing For the Best Only To Be Left with the Worst,

We Give Our All Each And Every day Praying That One Day they'll Love Us the Same:

Wishing And Hoping For Joy And Sunshine Instead Of Pain And Rain.

Why Do We Love Love, When Love Seems To Hate Us?

Love Hurts So Much Because All We Want Is To Feel Appreciated, Wanted, Needed and Cared For,

But Instead We Get Harsh Words, Tears And Slammed Doors...

Love Hurts So Much Because In Order To Love Someone You Must First Love Self,

Love Should Be Treasured like One's Wealth

Love Hurts So Much Because It's Interpreted Many Different Ways,

Love Hurts So Much Because the Definition Changes Every Single Day.

Love Shouldn't Hurt But Since It Does, You Have To Ask Yourself "How Could The One I

Gave My Heart To Break My Heart So Bad?"

So Gone Over You

So its officially over and I've never felt so bad in my life, I don't understand how something so good can turn into something so bad. Overwhelming mixed emotions are running through my head, I'm so confused and I don't know what to do.

Hot tears are running down my cheeks and my eyes are burning. I feel so incomplete and my mind feels empty. Without you I can't breathe like Mario and I don't wannabe without you like Aaliyah, I get so weak like SWV and I'm dangerously in love like Beyoncé. You just don't understand you're the chunky monkey to my Ben and Jerry's and the strawberry to my Fanta.

It's so hard to say goodbye like Boys II Men, I hope I don't catch amnesia like Cherish so I can forget the way you touched my body like Mariah Carey, Maybe one day I'll meet you at the crossroads like Bone-Thugs and Harmony, but for now I'm so gone like Monica.

Played Me/ Oops Sorry!

I hear soft Sounds

And I Smell Sweet scents

I feel your soft skin

And I kiss your luscious lips

I walk away mesmerized

With my hips slowly swaying

I'm sorry for tempting and teasing you I say as I walk out the door

You look at the door as it quietly closes

And think to yourself this crazy chick just played me.

Karma

It's So Easy Too Fall In Love, But So Hard Too Fall Out Of It... What Do You Do When

You're Whole World Falls Apart? Who Do You Turn Too When Your Life Starts Too Look

Real Dark? Where Does The Pain Settle? When Does The Rain Seem Too Stop? How Do You Stop The Breaks In Your Heart? When Does Happiness Seem Too Start? Who Does It Seem Too Come From? Questions That Clouded My Head Once the Love You Once Had For Me Was Found Dead..... Wasted My Time With The Lies, Sweet Nothings, And Passionate Kisses, Your Smooth Touches That Sent Chills Down My Spine...

Now There Just All Memories That Fill My Brain. I'm having a Jazmine Sullivan Moment Cause I Wanna Bust the Windows out Your Car, But I Don't Think That Will Help My Pain Cause I Don't Wanna Plead Insane. I Loved Yew Until You Gave My Heart A Break Now I Feel That You Weren't Anything But A Mistake. Real Recognize Real And Sweetheart You Are Now A Stranger. I Honestly Didn't See This One Coming, But It's Just GOD's Way Of Giving Me Space For Something Better, So In The End You

Gonna Be Bitter. You Messed With The Right One And You Thought I Was A B****

Well Wait Until You Meet Karma

Patiently Waiting

The Conversations and Stolen Glances, the Laughs and Silly Mishaps, the Time We Spend Together and How Secure You Make Me Feel, The Happiness, The Peace. The Constant Joy That Comes From Knowing You Have Me Patiently Waiting For The Time Too Come That I Can Call You Mine.

Patiently Waiting Until I Can Hug and Kiss You... Spend Endless Hours Talking, Cuddling, Hanging Out And Playing... Patiently waiting for the Moment When You Tell Me You're Ready to Fill the Empty Hole in My Heart, To Give My Love Life a New Start. Patiently Waiting To Be The One You Wanna Call When Your Down Or Just Need Somebody Too Talk Too... I'm Just Patiently Waiting For You To Be You And Me.

"Patiently Waiting."

Could It Be

I Pushed You Into The Back Of My Mind, Away From My Emotions And Feelings, Burying All Of My Lust And Love For You & In The Midst Of It All You Unexpectedly Pop Back Up...

A Plain Text Message With Just My Name Made All My Past Passion For You Burn

In My Chest... What Is It about You That Makes Me Wanna Leave the One I'm With. The

One That Treats I like I Should Be Treated, Could It Be Your Voice? Could It Be Your

Aggression? Could It Be Your Touch? Or Could It Simply Be That I'm Just Not over You?

It's Been Some Time That I've Wanted You & Just When I Thought I Was Done

Hungering for You My Affection Erupts In My Heart... I Have To Get You Out Of My

Head... I Honestly Thought The Infatuation With You Was Dead... Could It Be I Was

Lying Too Myself? Could It Be I Was Trying So Very Hard To Move On? Or Could It

Simply Be I Love You? Should I Drink Away My Sorrow? Drown It Out With Some Moscato? What

Do I Do? Because Chrisette Michelle Said It Best "All I Ever Think About Is You"... Could It Be I Need To Let All This Go? Could It Be That I Need To Tell You How I Feel? Or Could It Ever Simply Be?

Kris

Curves are something Vicious, mind is something dangerous, words stinging like a bee. I bet all thought I was talking about me... Sexualized by the way she's visualized... Naked to the staring eye, knowing there's more to her than her looks... Being approached differently has her mind kind of shook...

Wishing people could see past her pretty face hoping they can get a taste... Needing people to know her intellect without wanting to make her Sweat... Being shaped the way she is makes her feel deep regret... Cause she's a woman inside and out and she's one of the best...

-Fellas when you meet a woman meet her for her mind not her sex.

Cream

I once craved your touch, to me you used to mean so much. I used to tell you all my secrets but now I question the trust.

The sight of you once made my heart race, but now the beats are spaced… Your scent drove me crazy and I constantly called you my baby.

That's the past and when I think about how I was once obsessed I instantly get upset.

How can one man turn my whole world upside down and not give a damn? Have me fall in

love and then fall in love with someone else? Expect me to sit and wait until he gets his shit together?

I'll be damned, years invested in a dream, but he'll come crawling back when he realizes that these females can't love him like me because I'm the crop and the cream.

Not Knowing

Not Knowing What to Do To Make You Smile,

Not Knowing What to Do To Make You Laugh,

Not Knowing What to Do To Make You Love Me....

Not Knowing How to Make You Attracted To Me,

Not Knowing How to Talk To You about How I Feel,

Not Knowing How to Know If This Shit We In Is Even Real,

Not Knowing If the Words You Speak Are True,

Not Knowing If This Where You Want To Be,

Not Knowing If You Truly Love Me.

Not Knowing When We Could Have Old Days Back,

Not Knowing When We Could Get Back On the Same Track,

Not Knowing When You'll Love Me Again,

Not Knowing Is the Hardest Part..

Undercover Lover

The Day We Met Was a Day to Remember,

Kind Of Like the Day with the Prettiest Weather,

Voice like Smooth Velvet That Send Chills down My Spine,

Kisses To My Lips That Freeze Time And Confuse My Mind...

Lying Next To You Made Me Forget About the Troubles of the World,

You Had Me Feeling Like I Was Your Favorite Girl....

You Let Somebody Come Along And End Our Relationship. It Ended With A Twist...

You Left Me like A Joke Boy

But You Know I'm Nobody's Play Toy.

I Moved Onto The Next Vowing To Never Love Another Like I Loved You...

Then You Came Back But You're Gonna Have To Wait For Part 2

... To Be Continued

All I Know

Wishing We Could Go Back To The Old Days When We Were Both Happy : So In Love

And Making Plans About Starting A Family: Now Those Days Are Gone And Our Love Is

Fading To Black; Wanting To Walk Away But It's Hard Cause In The End I'ma Want You Back ...

What Do I Do And Where Do I Go From Here Because I Swear Another Bitch Loving You Is My Biggest Fear...

Baby I Need Some Understanding Cause My Mind And Heart Is Conflicting. What's On Your Mind, Do You Need Space Or Some Time?

Maybe I Should Pack up and Let You Clear your Mind; Spark a Blunt and Unwind.....

Wishing I Could Rewind And Go Back To When We Had Peace And We Would Actually Speak.

How Do I Let Go When Your Love Is All I Know?

Should I Go?

The Days of Loving You No Longer Exist,

Feelings Went Out The Window Quicker Than A Fugitive, Trying My Hardest Not To Cry And Break Shit, Heart Slowly Feeling Like It's About To Die And Quit.

Not Knowing What Else To Do or Say,

Nobody Can Take This Pain Away,

Wanting You to Say You'll Stay,

Knowing That Will Never Happen Turns My Blue to Gray. Should I Turn My Back On The One I Long For? Should I Close And Lock The Door? Should I Give Up On Something That Used To Be So Sweet?

The Person That Once Made Me Weak, Is Now The Same Person That Has Me Bleak.

He Used To Be My Sweet Dream And Now He's Nothing More Than A Beautiful Nightmare.

Hearing His Voice Makes My Heartstrings Tear And Brings Back Darken Memories Of Our Past Years.

Holding On To False Hope, Got Me Puffin' On Mad Dope. I Care For Him But I Want To Walk Away, Should I Go Or Should I Stay?

Broken Promises

Just When I Thought My Search For Love Was Over You Came Into My Life With Spoken Promises. Now My Search For Love Is Back On Because Of Your Broken Promises, The Lies You Told Broke The Bond That We Used To Hold, I Thought I Could Trust You With My Heart But Now You Got Me Sitting In The Dark.... I Wish You Would Have Been Real With Me Instead Of Lying Too Me && Making Me Fall For You...... I Thought I Loved You...

But Now I'm Sitting Here Looking Like a Fool.....I Should've Listened to the Ones That Told Me Too Stay Away && Find Somebody Better, But You Had Me So Weak Because Your Words Were So Sweet... I Knew I Shouldn't Have Trusted You By The Words You Speaking But My Heart Gave Me The Reason. You Were The One That Had My Heart & Mind On A String Like A Yo-Yo So You Could Drop Me Whenever You Felt The Need Too.

I Question Your Faithfulness Too Me, There Were Many Sins of Infidelity on Your Part, I Should've Known You Was No Good from the Start... But now it's All Over and I Must part... I'm Too Good For You, You Can Keep Your Spoken Promises That Turned Into Broken Promises &&. The Lies You Told

That Broke The Bond That We Used To Hold... Trust Me Your Gonna Miss Me & I'ma Be Long Gone.

There's No Love like Your First Love

You Kiss Her Thinking of Me, Knowing That I'm The One You Want, Your Insides Telling

You That I'm The One You Need...

You Touch Her Thinking That My Curves Are The One You Wanna Embrace. Your Mouth Grazes Hers When You Know My Lips Are The Ones You Wanna Taste...

Running Your Fingers Thru Her Hair Remembering When We Ran In The Rain And You Dried My Hair With Your Shirt.

Why Did You Have To Go And Make A Mistake Is The Question That Clouds Your Mind And Has You Messing With Rebound Chicks That Can't Match Even The Least Amount Of What I Have To Offer Too Yew....

Your Friends & Even Your Family Are Telling You That I'm Where Your Heart Is &. In The Back Of Your Mind You Know That They're Right...

You Sit Around & Read Old Text Messages & Letters That I've Written Too You & You Cry Knowing That Nobody's Gonna Love You Like I Love You...

The Way I Used To Make You Laugh, Smile, & Say My Name Is A Feeling That No Basic Broad Can Do Because There's No Other Like The One You Love...

Think about it for a Minute, Sit down and Reminisce. There's No One like Your First Love.

You

You.

Questions cloud my head as I think about the stress that was caused by loving you,

Emotions jumping around in my heart with unmade decisions of what to do about you,

Trying to wipe the Rembrandts of your kisses off my lips as I wash your scent off my skin,

Showering and letting the water rinse the feeling of your fingers out of my hair,

Playing love songs and shedding tears to release the pain of being betrayed by you,

Trying to get some sense of clarity of why you would wanna do me like this after all the things that we've said,

Sitting here trying to figure out when the love died and communication was lost,

Eyes looking glossy and I my salty tears are hitting my lips, praying inside my head asking for answers,

Ignoring text messages and phone calls from even my closest associates and loved ones, Not knowing what to do or say is making my heart hurt more with every word I type,

I guess I'ma just give you your space and try to get over the pain of losing you.

Hold On or Let Go

The Numerous Lies That I Have Been Told In My Relationships Make Me Feel Like I

Should Give Up On Love, But There's This Boy That Holds The Key To My Heart And I

Have To Have Him....I've Been Waiting For Him To Open Up His Pretty Brown Eyes And Look Around...

The Fire That I Get In My Eyes When I See Him Matches The Burning Desire That Builds Up In My Body When He's Away...

I Toss And Turn When I Dream Of The Passion That Could Be Created Between US...

It Kills Me That He Doesn't Realize That What I Say Is Real And I Mean Every Word That I Speak. My Love For Him Is Deeper Than Any Deep Blue Sea But Could Be Bittersweet As Any Salt Water Taffy...

I Just Need One Night Like Chris and Keri So I Could Tell Him And Show Him I Want To Spend My Life With Him Like Eric And Tamia... What Should I Do... Do I Hold On Or Let Go. Live. Laugh. Love.

Effortlessly Have you ever woke up feeling like you don't belong? Like all the odds are against you? Out of place and in a negative space? With the most confused look on your face, trying to piece together your feelings and darkest Secrets… Questions cloud your mind and your feeling like your running out of time…

Not knowing where to turn but not wanting to run… Run from your realization that your different from other people and you don't know how to express…

Express your feelings for the same sex… Holding this in for so long, wanting it to come out but not knowing which approach to take, at the same time not wanting to break.

Trying not to think and make your feelings shake… Questioning whether you should speak your truth or keep your silence… Keep this a quiet trial or make it a loud triumph… Worrying what your friends and family might say before remembering, "Only God Can Judge Me."

Live. Laugh. Love. Effortlessly

Black Memories

Memories of a happier time,

Back when there were no cries,

Silent passes and turning backs is what consumes us now...

No happy moments fill these halls,

And if these walls could talk,

There would be no words spoke...

Heart having mixed emotions,

Smoking too exhale the bullshit,

The bullshit of loving you,

Eyes flashing with visions of what I can be without you...

Waiting for the moment where I can fly free,

Stand on my own,

Free to the point where I won't sit and write about you.

Untitled

Broken dreams and unneeded desires, lingered kisses and silent shouts... Lusting for things unavailable and unseen, Sipping the lightest champagne as the mascara runs down my cheeks...

Thoughts of pleasure cloud my soul and devour my heart as the rain matches my infatuating pain... Hoping that you have a change of heart as my love for yew slowly fades to dark...

Fire fills my eyes as I start to shake, analyzing all your lies as my heart begins to break... I can't believe I fell for your pretty eyes and smooth words... My head erupts and my ears ring out your name, your scent is still on my skin and I finally realize I will never be the Barbie to your Ken.

What Is Love?

I don't understand the definition of love.

What is love?

Is love the feeling you get when someone special walks through the door?

Is love the way your heart skips a beat when they say your name?

What is love?

Is love the way you get happy when you see them?

Is love the tears you cry when they make you feel special?

What is love?

Is love the way your eyes light up when they look into your soul?

Is love the way you shiver when they kiss your lips?

Or is love the way I feel about you?

I think I'm in love.

Questions-Quotes

"How can the one I gave my heart to break my heart so bad? "What if I had a thing on the side, made you cry?" Other people tell me that I should let them love me so they can show me the way love's supposed to be. To be honest with you "I wish I never met you," because every time we talk I end up sayin' "Here we go again." Your voice used to be my "medicine"

But now "I'm ready to sign them papers." My ringtone used to be "Poison" and when I met

you, you asked "Can we talk for a minute." "Your love is like honey but mine is like "Whoa", "But if you take your love away from me I'll go crazy." I need a serious case of "Amnesia' to forget your "Love Jones." But I'm out of "Questions" & Now I'm walking down "Memory Lane."

Sincerely Signed

Trust me with your secrets and fears,

Believe me I'll be right there to catch your tears,

Tell me how you feel,

Always keep it real,

I'ma be by your side,

Just call me your ride-or-die,

I'll be there when you need to fight,

Or whenever you need to confide,

I'm hoping you can be my get-a-way

And take me to a place far-a-way

So we can keep our love packed inside

And we will never divide

Because true love is hard to find

But I think I found it with you

Sincerely Signed

-Shakerah

Walked Away

You woke up one morning and had different feelings towards the ones you once loved the most. The ones you sacrificed and lied for, the ones you vowed to lay down and die for.

What made you get up and walk away, forget all the things you used to say? Did love just die? Did you not care who would cry?

How could you just up and walk? Did you ever think how our world would turn dark? Children without a father figure, who's to guide us on this journey called life?

A mother without a husband. Lord please take away the strife. Father please help me understand how a man could just up and leave with no words to help us believe.. Could you help me figure out how you could just walk away?

Save Me

You Could Never Understand The Internal Pain I Go Through On A Daily Basis, The Feeling,

The Needing, No The Wanting To End My Entire Existence. The Everyday Changes Of My Mind, The Wanting To Be Alone All The Time. The Silent And Late Night Loud Cries.

People Only See How I Act On The Outside But Has Anybody Ever Stopped To Care Or Ask How I Feel On The Inside? Quick To Say "She Needs Meds" Instead Of "What's Bothering You?"

Judging Me From The Outside Hurting Me Deeper Than You'll Ever Know, I'm Not Seeking Attention, I Don't Act Depressed For Show. I Wish I Could Wake Up Everyday And Be Normal.

I Would Love Nothing More Than To Smile And Be Joyful, However I'm Battling With A Mental Disease With No Cure. I Would Love To Be At Peace But With Bipolar Depression Peace Is A Thing That's Never Sure.

Next Time You Look Down On Me Or Throw My Disorder In My Face, Understand That It Cuts Deeper Than Any Band-Aid Can Heal, Just Know That Most Days, It Gets Too Hard Too Deal. It's Like A Never

Ending Ocean And I'm Drowning In My Emotions With A Wish To Be Saved But Mental Thoughts Of Letting Go. You'll Never Understand The Internal Pain I Deal With Everyday And I'm Not Asking You Too, I'm Just

Asking That You Don't Turn Your Back On Me; Save Me.

Butterfly Exposed

"Even a Butterfly Can Have a Bad Side"

Making Love To The One You Love Is One Of The Best Feelings Ever.... Kissing Passionately

While Your Hearts Match Eachothers Beat.... Sweat Dripping Off Y'all Bodies While You Guys Entangle In Between The Sheets ...

Passion Flowing Through The Strokes And Motions, Sweet Words Being Whispered To Express Feelings And Emotions, Pain Is Pleasure And The Way You're Doing Me, I Pray You Wouldn't Love Anybody Else.

My Body Is Your Temple And Baby You Came To Worship... Love Is A Test And I Hope You Know That At Your Best You Are Loved....

My Heart Is Locked And I'm Hoping To Give You The Key.... But Before We Get There Let's Make More Love Between The Sheets.

Chocolate Bliss

Lips That Send Chills Down My Spine With A Glance,

Hoping One Day For A Chance,

A Chance To Taste Or A Simple Embrace,

A Smile That Makes My Body Hot,

Wanting You To Touch All The Right Spots,

Wishing I Could Spark Your Brain Over Stimulated

Conversation Listening To The Rain,

Wanting A Sip Of Your Hot Chocolate,

While You Make Me Cream,

Feeling Like I'm In The Middle Of A Wet Dream,

Needing You In My Reality,

Wanting To Make You Mine,

Desiring For A Minute Of Your Time,

Open To Getting In Your Bed..... I Mean Head;

Vying For A Kiss Or A Second Of Chocolate Bliss.

You Pick Me Up From Work And Notice That I Have On A Sundress With No Panties ... I Have

My Hair Down And Sunglasses On My Face.... I Tell You About My Day And Look At You

With Lust And Hunger And Say Who's Place....

You Reply Yours And I Lock The Car Doors

My Hair Goes Up And Then I Go Down,

You Moan "Oooh" As I Take You Softly. In My Mouth,

You Tangle Your Hand In My Hair,

I Take You Inch By Inch Never Coming Up For Air,

You Let Go Of My Hair And Reach Between My Legs,

All I Hear You Say Is "Damn Baby Your Soaking Wet".

I Feel You Explode In My Mouth And I Savor Every Drop, Next Thing I Know The Car Comes To A Sudden Stop.

I Sit Up And Realize We've Reached Our Destination. You Walk Around The Car And Open The Passenger Door… I Try To Get Out And You Push Me Down On The Floor…. You Slide

Your Face Between My Legs And Your Tongue In My Sweetness Until I'm Screaming That I

Can't Take Anymore…. I Tell You That I Want To Feel You Deep Inside….. But It Has Too

Happen. On The Inside …

We Go In The House And Before We Make It Past The Threshold You Have Stripped Both Of Our Clothes Off.... I Lead You To The Bedroom And Throw You On The Bed.... I Climb. On Top And Ride You Until We Both Get Our Rocks Off.

...Continued

Step Into My Bedroom, Dim The Lights, Pour A Glass Of Wine And Get Ready For The Time Of Your Life.

You Start To Wonder Where I Could Be As Erykah Badu Sings A Sweet Melody. I Text You And Tell You Too Blindfold Yourself: You Follow My Instructions Right Before I Walk Into The Room.

I Lay You On The Bed And Softly Kiss Your Lips As You Softly Rub On My Ass And Hips;

My Juices Start To Drip And I Get Up And Strip;

Passion Is Ripping Through My Body And I Want Nothing More Than You Inside Of Me; I Peel Your Clothes Off And Toss Your Blindfold To The Floor;

I Kiss Down Your Body Before Taking You Inch By Inch Into My Mouth.... I Suck You Nice And Slow While Usher Serenades Us, Candles Are Flickering Around The Room And It Starts To Rain;

We Start To Make Love And You Truly Give Me The Meaning Of Pleasure Is Pain; We Come In Unison; I Climb Off Of You And Roll A Splif As We Lay There Rolling In

Ecstasy.

Closure

Dear Aunt Kim…

Sitting here trying to not to question God, but I can't stop thinking, "Why?" Why could he take the one we needed most, the one who kept us close? Trying to fight back the tears as I sit here and remember all the memories throughout the years. Listening to music that reminds me of you, hoping it will get me through. A smile grazes my face as I think of all the grace you embraced.

Reminiscing about all the lessons you taught me and the aura of respect you embodied. Your time with us was cut short and all I've been feeling is hurt. How am I supposed to go on without you? I can't believe this happened and my mind won't wrap around you not being here. Honestly, dear, that was my greatest fear…

We needed you close, but God needed you closer, but how and when are we supposed to get closure?

Rest In Peace

Kimberly Denise Brown

March 22, 1971 – March 30, 2017

My Aunt Kim

www.ingramcontent.com/pod-product-compliance
Lightning Source LLC
Chambersburg PA
CBHW071544080526
44588CB00011B/1783